# Inspiring POEMS TO FEED YOUR Soul

MATTHEW COOK

authorHOUSE®

AuthorHouse™
1663 Liberty Drive
Bloomington, IN 47403
www.authorhouse.com
Phone: 1 (800) 839-8640

Published by AuthorHouse 03/03/2017

Library of Congress Control Number: 2017903235

ISBN: 978-1-5246-7456-4 (sc)
ISBN: 978-1-5246-7455-7 (e)

Print information available on the last page.

This book is printed on acid-free paper.

# Contents

# Shinning Star

You are still so young and may not yet understand just how much we care. When you get older, we hope you remember that we were always there.

There to witness the drive you had to be the best at whatever you do. There to know how sweet your smile when we took those pictures of you.

That giggle that sounded so cute since before you could even walk, your curious questions that began with "why", when you first began to talk.

Nearly seven years have passed since you first came along, and our hearts are still filled with joy, like an old familiar song.

Pillow fights with Pop Pop, and cuddling with Nana Sue, all the moments spent just being so close to you.

You are the child in our lives that brings a feeling of youth to our being. The fresh innocence of life within you that we are constantly seeing.

You will grow older and your interests will become more mature. Your life will be magnificent, this I know for sure.

Always remember sweet child that we love you more than life itself, your pictures will be standing proudly on your Grandparents shelf.

For you Logan, we give you our hearts, so that as you go out in the world with a part of our souls, you will feel our loving spark.

# The Gift

The gift of life we all are given, can be easily lost from our sight. The struggles we face in our everyday lives can make us wonder if it's worth the fight.

Our New York seasons that tease us with warmth, then dump snow on our fresh mowed yards. Things we never planned on, or never looked ahead that far.

Well, life can be a bitch sometimes but one thing we know for sure, if we hurried through all the times like those, life would be a blur. The challenges we face make us who we are and give us the scars that define our place in the gift of life we all are given, can be easily lost from our sight. The struggles we face in our everyday lives can make us wonder if it's worth the fight. Our New York seasons that tease us with warmth, then dump snow on our fresh mowed yards. Things we never planned on, or never looked ahead that far.

Well, life can be a bitch sometimes but one thing we know for sure, if we hurried through all the times like those, life would be a blur. The challenges we face make us who we are and give us the scars that define our place in time. Our fortunes shine brighter beside those scars, because we survived despite those crimes.

Spring is here to lift our spirit, even though It's still makes us shiver. It may take a glass of wine or two to stimulate your liver. Just live your life in a positive way to make each day all worthwhile.

Take the time to make someone smile, let them know that's just your style. The gift of life is fragile and short, and should always be given a chance. It can be beautiful to explore, but never just at a glance.

Take a deep breath and let it our slow, close your eyes and caress your soul. Life remains a promise to none, so go outside and have some fun!

# Flashback

When a song brings back a memory from a page back in your life, do you sense how long ago that was, or do you live it like it was today. Should it always seem those times so dear were lived so far away.

Those songs written in better times had some thought and purpose in mind, much different than many songs today that have very few lyrics I find.

A new generation has taken hold, a mindless perception I fear, has changed the depth of song writing from the old songs I hold so dear.

There are a few that take the time to create a tasty melody, or perhaps a story to be told. Songs to hold the interest of both the young and the old.

However, many just try to just pump out something so incredibly fast, they forget the effort it takes to create something that will last.

I would like some songs created now to complement this point in time, some memories I can upload at some future moment in my mind.

Music has always been a bookmark to remind you of younger days. It soothes your soul and expands your mind in so many different ways.

My only fear is that the only bookmarks I may remember will be the ones from way back, due to the downward trend of songs today, and the amount of soul they lack

Let's all hope there will be some change and more stories will be told. I hope it's soon, since many of us continue to get old. Peace!

# Her Children

A gathering of souls has walked through a door, none of them knowing just what was in store.

They have come to a place not familiar at first, but can still relieve their hunger and quench their thirst.

Brought together by the most loving one, and are blessed again by her loving son. A new home for them, as a promise and a part of her will, he knew he had a job to fulfill.

This family stays now as one, her children will sleep and play as together, their new lives have begun They are part of a legacy that our mom left on this earth, an extension of love that she shared from her birth.

These souls remind us of what she did to keep them safe and warm, and how important life is in whatever the form. Keep them safe my brother, I know your heart is in that place. I know up in heaven there is a smile on mom's face.

# Mrs. Right

Looking for Mrs. Right is the hardest job I've got.
Day to day it's the same old thing, haven't found a lot.
Out there somewhere, my lady's around the bend.
Just looking for that someone special, just looking for a friend.

Hoping for a soul to share all that life could offer us, or
Someone to ask about my day, or just to make a fuss.
I need a girl to call my own, to show her all my love,
As much as the sun from time to time, to shine down
from above.

Looking for Mrs. Right is not as easy as it seems,
Or finding that perfect one you see deep within your dreams.
To only find the one for me, I know I'd be complete,
Just hope I don't have to wait too long before we both can meet.

Hoping for a partner to make sweet love to me.
To fill that empty place inside that only she can see.
I need a girl to fill my heart with happiness and feel whole,
This I pray to end this pain, and fill my empty soul.

# The Power Of Love

What is it that opens your eyes to a lonely stray dog on the street? The homeless man on that park bench looking for something to eat. Those feelings which are so inherent deep within our core, might cure all the suffering and give meaning to compassion and understand what it's for.

The value of our own lives that we feel everyday should mirror how we perceive all life the very same way. For we all exist from the first heartbeats of our birth, in God's eyes we share the exact same worth.

Life is precious, as it is a gift given for a very short period of time. How we choose to live it can be dark and bitter or taste as sweet as wine. The difference is up to ourselves, as each of us has the power to decide.

We can use the power of love to continue, and push all the hate aside. If you can love yourself and realize that everyone deserves to live, there might always be a reason to feel empathy, to forgive.

This may not be easy, as our world has been torn so far apart. But, in order to have peace, we must understand where to start. Peace begins with a simple respect of life in whatever may be the form. This taught to our children to be the decisive and absolute norm.

Somehow this notion has become forgotten, and our children have gone astray. We see this on the news through all the violence we see everyday. Black against white, and white against black, it still comes down to the compassion we lack.

To care about each other and what we might give to ease all this pain, can eventually teach the world what showing a little love just might gain. Again, I make a plea to all that may feel they could listen, to create a world in our lifetime that could finally endure and perhaps even glisten.

# A Birthday In Heaven

I hope they celebrate birthdays in heaven Mom, we remember it still every year. All we have here on earth, are the memories we hold so dear. You can sit down with Dad, both your parents and his parents too! Have some cake and ice cream and open those presents for you.

This day will always have meaning to everyone you ever touched. Your absence here has left an empty space, and we all miss you so very much. Your spirit lives on in heaven and within many souls here on earth. I know now the value of what our faith in God is worth.

Someday we will meet again, to be with all the souls we have ever loved. For now, I will take comfort that have an Angel floating above.
Happy birthday mom, say hello to everyone there, you will always exist inside my heart, and your love still flows everywhere!

# Christmas In Heaven

There are those of us on this special day that are missing someone they love. We wonder how they are doing as they walk in the heavens above.

It may not be the same as we open our presents this year, thinking about the person we miss and the memories we hold so dear. I know in my heart that they feel the same way as the kook down from that special place, a tear from heaven fans to earth as it rolls down off their face.

But heaven holds a peaceful bliss that comforts them each day. Although we miss them here on earth, they exist in a painless way.

Their Christmas is spent with others they love as well as Jesus himself. That thought is just as special as their picture kept on a shelf. We may be saddened by the absence and it may be sometimes hard to face, but take comfort that they live on in that very special place.

I spend this Christmas knowing that my mom is still close to me, happy that she is spending her Christmas in a place she longed to be. Together with my father and experiencing the peace of heaven above, I will celebrate the birth of Jesus as I send her all my love.

# My Christmas List

People to find a place in their hearts for all living creatures, no matter who they might be, or how different their features. A world free of hate would sure be nice, the cost of freedom that would have no price.

Cancer to be cured for all time, no more fear of dying for yours and mine. A revelation of peace to rain down on this earth, an understanding of our own self worth.

The homeless to have a place to call home, orphans to know they are never alone.

Hunger to be a word that does not exist, an open hand instead of a fist. These are the things that bring meaning to this season. Wrapping gifts in a box is not the real reason.

This time of year would have never begun without the birth of our Lord's only son. Forget not the sacrifice he made, so that his teachings in our hearts will never fade.

Merry Christmas to you all, and may you hold a place in your souls, to show the strength of his words to enlighten and unfold.

# Christmas Dear

Having a family at Christmas is the very best time of the year. Time spent with all those you hold so dear. It's because I met you and became your only man, I was given this gift of family as I cherish this ring on my hand.

Without you I would not know the love in my life that comes by having you as my wife.

Along with all the sweet things that you do, the way you care about me through and through.

This gives me a reason to hold you so dear, especially at this special time of year.

You gave me two son's that came with this deal, they have given me that sense of family that feels so real.

It's because of you that there is a Grandson in our lives, he has been so special to me when I look in his eyes.

I never thought I would feel all these things in my life, and it is all become possible because you became my wife. I love you so much for making me whole, for giving me a purpose, for warming my soul.

Merry Christmas, my love, as we enjoy this season. For as I smile right now, I know that you are the reason!

# Reflections

Thinking about all that has transpired over this last year, believe it is time to reflect. Things that we had control over in our lives, as well as those we did not expect.

Is it not how we react to what comes down our way, that defines how we all might act or what kind of things we all might say. I think much of our reactions could turn out so much better, and in a more constructive design, if we thought out our intentions. Perhaps a different result we would find.

There is such little point in stressing how different an idea can be from what you may seek, when it is the differences between us that makes each one of us unique.

Being all the same is not what this country was meant to be. A blend of people from all over the world have poured in from sea to sea. I am part German,

Scottish, Irish, and more. I call myself an American, because this is the Land that I adore.

People may protest in order to make their opinions known, as that is a right they can surely hold true. However, in doing so they can not infringe on any of the rights given to me and you.

Peace can be achieved if everyone listens as much as they speak. Have compassion for those less fortunate, stop preying on the weak. We are about to celebrate a day of Thanksgiving, to be thankful for something that enhances our state of living.

Let us be thankful that we are free, that we have a potential to be good. Within our souls there are past generations of spirits that really know we should.........

# Post Election Thoughts

As expected after any election, there are people who are happy, and those who are not. There are always winners and losers within the confines of this kind of scenario. What matters to our country's welt being is just how everyone handles this transition

You can accept what has happened as a natural process of a democratic society and resume your life as a law abiding citizen, Or, you can resist the inevitable and continue to protest what has transpired. This is your choice as an American as wen, and you may do as you wish. Although it may be appropriate to acknowledge exactly what would be gained in doing so.

The election is over. The majority of the people have spoken, and it is time to move into the next business at hand. That is to unite as Americans to start another four years under a new and different leadership. This is nothing new in our country. Nothing that has not happened time and time again. How we deal with this transition will describe within our history, as to what kind of people we are here in this particular century. Historians will certainly be taking note, as it is our first president to take office that is not a politician or has ever served in the military. There may be advantages to this as our government has been in need of some shaking up, or at the very least, some drastic change in it's desire for greed and corruption.

In any event, he will be in charge and there will be changes in our government as a result* Again, nothing new here as well, It is up to us as American citizens to embrace the inevitable, to understand that change is the basic aspect of every natural situation on this earth. It is how we adapt to change that defines just how much more civilized we have become.

Be hateful and violent and you regress into a realm of fear that only belittles our efforts to be more than we are Be kind, compassionate, and retain a sense of positivity toward a more productive goal, and our country can proclaim the excellence that I believe can define us into the future.

It is time for all of us to come together as members of a designation called "The human race" A promise of pride in our commitment to better ourselves through love and compassion. This should be the cry of the masses. Of course, this is only the opinion of one proud American toward his fellow American's to express a dream of peace that one day we can all stand together and simply be thankful for the freedom this country provides.

# Perceptions

It's been a while my friends, my thoughts locked in my dreams. Not always easy to express just how I feel it seems. Life has brought on a new chapter to unfold, a difference between my past and new stories to be told. Looking forward as an orphan I see my future in a different way. The memories of my youth bring forth the precious joy of a much simpler day.

Now as age has given a perspective that we all must face, I find myself living in a much more challenging place. Not everything falls within the realm of what we perceive, truth does not always reflect what we want to believe.

We strive to understand the meaning of what path life should take us, as we venture down that road. Should we take that path alone, or share that heavy load.

I have found so far that life takes on a special meaning, when you share that path with a host of different beings. Be it animals or man, the list can go on forever. Sharing your existence brings meaning to each endeavor.
The world is made up of the living and spirits from the past, we should all do our part to make each of our legacies last. Make the spirits of our loved ones be proud of how we live, and those who we share this world be thankful for what God can give!

# The Bonding

I have bonded with a new soul it seems, and although it's only a cat, I do not take this lightly it is merely a matter of fact. He looks at me with those piercing blue eyes and captures my very soul. I see this tiny creature as a living being to behold. He lays on my chest and stares at me as if to ask if he will be alright. In a gentle voice a tell him he is safe with me tonight. A luck boy he finds himself in a home which has years of love. A tradition started from my mom who now lives high above.

It starts again, as a soul to save from an otherwise savage land. It always has brought me so much joy to stretch out a helping hand.

He will join us now as many others have, to live out his life in peace. He is small right now, but soon I know he will be a fine little beast.

He is the third one I've had of Siamese desent, as the first two lived nearly 20 years each. It feels so good to have another and to now join his sister's Angel and Peach.

I know there are those out there that understand these words that I speak. The special bond between man and beast that fills your home with all the love you may seek.
This new soul that has graced my life in such a short amount of time, has put a smile on the face of that heavenly mother of mine.

# To My Mom

Thank you Mom for helping make my life feel so complete. From giving all your good advice, to a lot of the cats beneath my feet. You have been my friend and so much more, I am blessed more than I know. I'm so lucky to have a Mom like you with all the kindness that you show. When I hear your name out around the town, it's mentioned with high regard. You have brought so much love to folks, when life can be so hard. Thank you for all the times you've prayed for me Mom, I feel safer every day. It warms my heart to know that you care for me that way.

You're the best you know, an Angel sent from high above. For all these things you will always have a son's undying love. God sent you here to make this world a better place to live. The animals in his kingdom all know of the love you give. Always know how much you mean to us, whether be man or child or beast. No matter how bad the world might seem, we can be thankful for you, at least. I love you Mom and always will, cause you're the one who cares the most. The amount of joy you have given the world could stretch from coast to coast,

# Remembering You

A year has passed since you have gained those Angel wings. Lots of time to reflect back at so many wonderful things, from experiencing the pain of child birth to bring me the breath of life, to walking down the isle as you watched me take vows with my wife.

So many memories are flashing through my mind, this woman who had so much compassion, whose sole purpose was to be kind. I never met someone who gave so much of herself as she lived everyday through every year. This is why I miss her so much, why I've shed so many tears.

She touched so many lives with her many selfless acts as she walked this earth with grace. She left a hole in al! our hearts as she left this empty space. However, Heaven gained this Angel and she now floats with all the souls who found peace, both people who have passed and every single kind of beast.

She was the matriarch of our family, very strong and tough as nails, but was softened by a simple purr or a wag of a furry tail. Mom would do anything to help someone in need. Always hoping that the rest of the world would someday plant that seed.

Thank you mom, for giving us a sample of how beautiful the world could be, if only everyone could understand the love that you could always see. Compassion and empathy for those found in harms way, can be joined together and find peace in this very simple way.

She had a message for the world to someday understand, that love binds all cultures, all religions across these great lands, her wish was for peace, that all could live with no fear. For these tireless efforts her spirit remains near.

You have passed to another realm and I am so proud to have known such a soul, tied so close to my being. When I look up towards heaven, it will always be an Angel that I'm seeing. Anita Marie, as you dance in that stage up above, always know you have my undying and eternal love.

Your Son
Matthew Douglas Cook

# What Is Wealth

Wealth is a concept, not a state of financial bliss. It is the accumulation of something many people tend to miss. To some it would be lots of cash to receive, to make them feel rich is what they believe.

To others it pertains to something much more real, an acquired gift of friendship which is something you can feel. If more of this sensation was felt around our lives, such peace could exist in a world full of lies.

We all try to obtain what makes us happy inside, during these uncertain times that span far and wide. Material things which may seem so fulfilling, only cloud your mind of the joy you are missing.

The feeling of love and knowing someone cares, is worth more than all best clothes you could ever want to wear. People are worth more than any concept of what thing you may possess. Compared to a person the value is much less.

This unique concept is what could change how the world is conceived today. To change the value of what is important to life in this way. Everything is judged as how this thing can benefit me. Oil, land, you know of all these things we see.

Would it not make sense to hold the same value to all the living flesh that lives and breathes more than the simple objects and shiny things that we all perceive.

The concept of life is a value that has been so often set aside, as we are drawn to the illusions of what money can buy. The best kind of wealth each of us could possibly bring to unfold, is the blessing of many friends to embrace and to hold.

The gathering of hands clenched around this world in peace, will ensure a friendship of man so that all wars could cease. Power to the people could be a warrior's cry for all the races of this earth. For it is the reason for our ultimate worth!

# A Simple Thought

Sometimes I sit and gather a pen, and write down a thought that i am thinking again.

But this thought that I am trying to find is somehow stuck in the back of my mind. It is not something I can feel or touch, or anything that really matters that much.

It's something I know I can quickly write down, but I just can't transfer this thought That I've found. Maybe it's not a thought at all, could it be I'm not quite on the ball?

I know now this thought I'm trying to write down, is not a thought.....but only a sound.

# A Truck Driver's Daydream

It was a cold dark day in an overcast mood, just another voyage, my truck...myself and who??

Sometimes on these dark days with often to signs of relief, I feel as though I'm not alone, but no one there to see.

Looking about my cab I find, there's no one to be found. But still I can't stop wondering what I feel all around. I really don't care, it's only a feeling. It could be anything wild or alien.

One day I was trucking down 17, when I noticed that feeling coming on strong. My heart beat fast, adrenalin ran free, I knew that feeling could not be wrong.

began to fade, like an invisible man and sink into the depths of this oversized van. The engine soon matched it's R.P.M's with my heartbeat and I soon felt every bend. l was a part of this truck in every way. Time spent there was like a century of days.

But, all this time I could not see, the truck, the road, or even me! Who was driving, who could stop? Apparently I couldn't do a lot. Sooner or later I would run out of gas, a cop would stop or a wrecker would pass.

All of a sudden I felt a big jerk and a screech, and then we slowed down. The truck had stopped* and to my surprise was the sound of a forklift and the chorus of two guys.

Matt's back they said, but little did they know, that the guy they once know, was not going to show. They opened up the door and looked all around, and looked puzzled at what they had found. All that was there was a truck it seemed, could it be the driver was just unseen?

Jeff sat there a minute with the radio on, changing channels and adjusting the tone. Turning to John could hear him say, don't you just feel like you're not alone?

# Election Time

Election year...here we are again. Do we have the same views, will you still be my friend?

We all see everything written on sites such as these, so concerned about just who we should please. Some of us stray left as others are drawn to the right. Truth becomes twisted and fades away from our sight.

What you hold true to your convictions defines exactly who you are. What you hear on the airways can only influence you so far. You must commit to your conception of right and wrong, the outcome of this election with only last so long.

The way you feel about what this great country means to you, fuels the compassion that you understand about the red, white, and blue. Freedom, choice, and the beauty of this land has given many an American a reason to stand!

So much blood has been shed to defend what we all hold so dear. The notion that all men and women can decide their own fate and never live in fear. This cannot be the end of a country so grand, nor can corruption or greed betray the glory of this beautiful land.

The choice has always been ours, as the people within that doctrine that we all hold so dear. Our Constitution holds the answers that only the corrupt and wicked leaders will eventually fear.

Peace and prosperity will come to those who respect the law of the land, and are not afraid to take that ultimate stand. Believe in ourselves as a blend of the best from all over this earth. The strength of this nation needs a vital rebirth.

We must break away from what has become the normal way of things, and embrace a different path for America that only honesty, faith, and courage can.

Corruption must be overthrown, while greed is cast aside, a concept of "WE THE PEOPLE ", must be the cry of our side. Not Right, or Left, but a unity of the American soul, will make this country a paradise to behold!

# Mom

The most incredible person you will ever know is the one that brought you into this place. She held you in her loving arms, and wiped the tears from your face.

Such sacrifice this woman has given all her days, to care for her children in so many ways. Working so hard to make sure we were fed, tucking us in when it was time for bed.

As we all grew older she still worried almost everyday, but it was time we moved on, we could no longer stay. It was time we all had to leave the nest. She would cry a little and wish us the best. We begin our own lives and keep our moms in our hearts, never forgetting how we all got our start. Dinners on Sundays with Mom and her cooking, always letting her know how young she was looking. Although time is something that sneaks up on us so fast even though we hope her love will outlast.

Cherish every moment of a mom's life that she shares. Thank her for giving you her time to care. She gave us life and a future. Mom kept us safe and warm. She gave us love in the most purest form.

From the moment you were born till she takes her last breath of air, she will always be there for her every child when life can be unfair. An unconditional love that we depend on when she is here. That same love that we miss when we shed that final tear,

For some of us Mom is watching from a higher place. still caring and loving while we remember her familiar face. For us she is an Angel in heaven just like she was on this earth, and we will always be thankful for the blessing of our birth.

# A Night's Fire

A gentle flame ignites my fire as I wait for the sun to fall from the sky. The air cools and dusk arrives, the sparks from the embers begin to fly.

Tranquility flows quietly and fills the air with a peaceful bliss. The fire begins to illuminate the night and calms me like a gentle kiss.

Soon friends arrive to join into this special place in time, we find a union of minds as we enjoy a taste of wine. We speak of youthful times when life was fresh and new.

We laugh at all the crazy things that we all used to do. But most of all we cherish these simple joys of living, just to look in awe at the bright full moon, or to feel the warmth that this fire was giving.

Even as the hot coals warm us to the bone and the friendships we feel thrive like flames into the night, it is the power of God's creations that keeps this tranquility firmly within out sight. As we look into the deepness of the night sky as it blankets our peaceful realm, we feel a presence that keeps this real. It's not only something that we can see without eyes, but a love of life that we can feel.

Embrace these moments, as we never know how few or how many, I just know each is worth every penny!

# Soul Searching

Flames flicker in the darkness as I search my soul, finding peace and a feeling of purpose is my goal.

I look up to the stars as if I could conceive heaven up in the sky, knowing that this world is a dimension deep within you and I.

We search for a truth or a reason we carry on in a world that has no promises to keep. I fry to enjoy the sweetness of what life can give before I go to sleep.

When we wake up we thank the Lord for that gift he gives, as we start another day to enjoy another day to live. How precious it is to feel the taste of this earth, as we continue each day from that distant day of our birth.

Treasure my friends as we all continue to breathe, of the beauty of existence to which is a privilege, I believe.

Help your brothers and sisters as they struggle through whatever life may bring, for they may never be given the gift to survive the unexpected things.

Peace, Love, and compassion are the three realities that cures all and heals the wounds of those who are in need. It may be up to all of us to plant that special seed.

I bring this message as just a brother of man that maybe someday more people may understand. What will reunite this world will be a force from up above, what will ignite that reality is the power of love.

# Summer Nights

WE HEAR THE WHISPER OF THE FIRE AS IT BURNS AT OUR FEET, WE SPEAK OF ALL THE OLD TIMES AS OUR BODIES FEELS THE HEAT.

WE STAND BACK AS SPARKS BLOW THROUGH THE CRISP NIGHT BREEZE, ALL THE DAYS TENSIONS ALL SLOWLY BEGIN TO EASE.

THE DARKNESS ABOVE ENHANCED BY STARS SHINNING SO BRIGHT, BRINGS SUCH A BLANKET OF SOLITUDE ONTO THE SHADOW OF NIGHT.

PEACE HAS NOW CONSUMMED OUR PRESENCE IN THIS AWESOME PLACE. OUR EXISTENCE STANDS SO STILL WITH IN TIME AND SPACE.

WHEN WE PART FROM THIS WE HAVE SHARED SOMETMNG RARE, A SPECIAL FEELING THAT WE ALL TAKE FROM THERE.

THE BOND THAT IGNITES LIKE THE FIRE THAT BURNS IN THE NIGHT, WILL BRINGS US BACK AGAIN BEFORE THE NEXT MORNING LIGHT.

THIS MOMENT THAT TOUCHES THAT SENSE OF BEING FREE, THAT PERSPECTIVE OF WHAT LIFE IS SUPPOSE TO BE, ESCAPES US WE FORGET TO CHERISH THESE TIMES, IT IS THE PEACE OF WITHIN THIS SPACE THAT BINDS.

TAKE THE TIME TO SHARE YOUR LIFE WITH YOUR FRIENDS, SO THAT THE FIRE IN YOUR SOULS WILL NEVER END.

# A Birthday For An Angel

Born on this day on a different December, came an Angel to which I will always remember.

Her name will forever sound so very sweet to me, of course that name is Anita Marie. Such a blessing from her kindness that touched so many lives, her absence now still brings tears to my eyes.

A tender day that will approach every year, as I remember the birthday of my Mother so dear. We still speak to her daily, my family and I, we pray that she is listening as each day passes by. I know God always had a plan for her, perhaps to care for all the souls in heaven with four legs and fur. Much of her life was spent

Saving as many creatures as she could, not just because she loved them, she just always thought she should. This was her calling as her heart showed compassion every single day. There was never anyone in need she could ever turn away.

As each year goes by and this day in December is remembered for her selfless deeds, we should all try to carry on her spirit by helping others in need.

I carry her spirit deep within my heart, as I continue along with my life. I feel closer now to my brother, 1 value more the love of my wife,

We all carry on when we lose someone we cherished in so many ways, it's how we keep remembering them that will help us through our days,

Anita Marie was my Angel on earth when she walked among us and God's creatures. Now she is an Angel in heaven as I remember her beautiful features.

Watch over me Mom, as 1 know you always have done, I will now and forever be your loving son.

# Born Again

An angel has found her wings today, God has lifted her from this earth. She gave this world all her love and kindness, she blessed me with my birth.

I know in my heart she is at peace up above, we give her our thoughts and send all our love.

God took the time to set up the stage that will give her the room to dance, she is stretching now and standing tall as she takes that perfect stance. May the angels be your partner mom, as you glide across that floor, an audience in heaven will be applaud and adore.

You will be in my heart forever and a big part of my soul to me, I am a product of your love and the man I will always be.

# A Roadie's Life

We are the first to arrive with a wrench in our hand, ready to set up a show or a band.

There are trucks to unload, ramps to bring down, the bang of the steel is a familiar sound.

Soon we will carry down all the heavy things that together will make these halls to sing.

Road cases roll toward a stage not yet erected, into a place that our boss has selected.

Aluminum truss constructed above, bolted together in a labor of love.

Miles of cable are brought into play, to connect all lights and the sound for the day.

More and more, bigger is better, the riggers hang from the sky and a tether. All of this done with a passion to create, to build something cool then sit back and wait,

We wait for that time at the end of our day, when we have to tear it down and put it away. The smell of hot wires and the pain that we feel as we gather up all these cases and strap in the steel.

It's all worth it though when the work is done, we still all manage to have some fun. Balls of gaff tape flying in the air, always the smell pizza somewhere.

Four hours bringing it in, two hours taking it out. All for a couple hour show, or there about.

It is what it is, as we always say, our motto to live by to get through the day.

A roadies life is not for the faint of heart, as you can see, but a roadies life it will always be!

# A New Year

Another year has come to an end as most are glad it's over. Now it's time to decide if to end it drunk or maybe sober. Some of us will fight off sleep, so to watch that ball come down, while many go out into the night to act much like a clown.

Don't get me wrong, both are fun and I have enjoyed each over the years. It's always a treat to go out with friends to have some wine, or drinks some beers. We reflect on our lives during this current year and make resolutions for the year ahead. We celebrate and all hope to make it safely back to bed.

Soon we start another year to begin all over again. Everyone hoping it's a far better one as we try to look around the bend. Perhaps we could think of a reality that most of us may forget, a way to fear no future, or to have no real regrets.

The most important time we all must learn to desire, is the here and now that exists. It's the only time we each have the power to enjoy life within our midst.

We can never relive the past, and the future is not ours to control.

Right here and right now is our time to shine and our happiness to behold,

Be safe my friends, as you celebrate a new year passed. I value you all in my life, because right now goes by so fast!

# A Peaceful Fire

I feel a cool breeze on a night in early spring. Pondering the kind of pleasure a nice campfire might bring.

The smell of maple as it burns in the dark, the ambers as they fly like wings on a spark. I feel the warmth flowing outward from the light, as I sense the peaceful quiet of a cool spring night.

The coals form like red ice cubes among the neatly stacked logs, as the smoke swirls into an infinite fog.

Tranquility fills the air as I look up into space, my heart feels the peace and is consumed by this place.

As I watch my fire dance off each and every branch, I thank the lord above that I still have this chance. A peaceful time to enjoy a simple thing, like the soulful release only a fire can bring.

# My Rock

When I rise in the morning I thank God for that chance, to see that familiar face and share an early glance.

A kiss goodbye as we start our day, another I love you is what we always say. I think about her as lunchtime comes to pass, a phone call to her time goes by so fast.

We share our day as we come home to rest, we comfort ourselves, like two birds in a nest. When the night grows near we climb into bed, we feel the warmth as we lay down our heads.

I wake up the next day to thank God again, the woman I married is still my best friend.

# Souls To Touch

Each of us walk down a path in life to encounter whatever we may find, some seek what the senses desire, others nurture their minds.

As I think of what I look for the most, eventually a certain reality unfolds.

The real lasting impressions are connections with so many souls.

It is something inside each of us that defines just who we are. Not the shell that surrounds us, but our spirits by far.

We each possess a uniqueness that sets us apart from the rest. Something to shine so brightly when we strive to be our best, This is the soul that every form of life was given to share. To interact with each other, with souls everywhere.

I feel these sensations with those who I meet, either standing upright, or those curled up by my feet. Animal souls are the most unique of them all, as their loyalties are as intense as a lonely wolfs call.

To touch as many souls in a lifetime as we can, will only enhance the many encounters that we may meet in that distant land.

Take time to look into the souls that you meet. Appreciate all for what they too. may seek. We are all created from the dust of the earth, each is destined for a purpose from the moment of birth. Respect each others time we have for our hearts to beat, for it is our souls someday, that God will finally meet.

# Remember

In the land of freedom an eagle flies above, he circles the heavens to protect the land we love,

Men and women from across this fertile land, lay down their lives every day, so now we all must lend a hand.

We do this by respecting the values our forefathers set down, the constitution that was written when patriotism abound.

To remember that our flag was to be looked at with respect. That a feeling of country should be in our hearts to reflect.

It is not easy to keep our land so free, there are evil minds that not everyone can see. Respecting the freedoms of the common man may not always be recognized by the corporate stand.

Greed and envy will bring a challenge to us all, by keeping this evil from making this great nation fall. The thoughts of our founders were to keep the PEOPLE in charge, to forge a democracy that keeps our freedom in sight.

it is this philosophy that makes it all worth the fight.

Let us bring back the feeling that our country is still proud, that our message of freedom is spoken strong and loud.

God bless this land and may we all live here free, we must all love this country from sea to shining sea!

# A Simple Truth

True happiness should come from a place in your heart that makes a difference for someone else, that sets yourself apart, Wealth and material things are temporary at best, what you may think makes you happy just to be like the rest.

What brings the most joy to anyone's soul is to see what the act of giving can do to make our lives whole.

Cherish the time you have with your friends, as we never know if we will see them again.

Embrace the sun, the wind, and the rain, for these are forms of pleasure that only on earth will remain.

Simple things in life bring the most meaning when times get you down, and it's the close people in your life that you will always want around.

True wealth will come from the friends that you find, they will comfort your soul and enhance your mind,

We were all created to live here in peace, that should ring forever in our souls. I pray for all someday, to have that ultimate goal.

# What Do You Believe

What do you believe, is a question you often hear, what are your political views, what do you fear. You see this often as you are searching the net, and even sometimes ponder your beliefs,

It depends on where you are, on how you are able to sound out. Those who cannot live free may know what I'm talking about. There are those who want you to think along the same lines as they want you to do, not caring if that is something that might not be agreeable with you.

This is something that has occurred for a very long time, for thousands of years beliefs have been different between yours and mine. Mutual respect may be the path we might seek, to understand we are different no matter if you are strong or weak.

People should believe what they want, but leave you alone, and respect that you have beliefs of your own. To force yours on anyone's space, is why there are conflicts in the first place.

These are views our forefathers wrote down, it was called a constitution, and by it we are bound. We live in a land that was meant to be free. To let all of you be you and for me to be me.

I can think of no other way to be simple and clear. Our country was created so that we no longer live in fear. Respect one another and strive to show some love, for we were founded through our God up above!

# Father

I think back of a time when you were part of this world, a person I looked forward to see. A strong man with a brilliant mind, someone who I always hoped could someday be.

He brought us from a distant land to settle us in a house of his own. I felt the warmth of his smite as he looked down at me, along with his love I have always known.

He worked very hard to give a good life to his wife and boys each day, when all I knew back then was to go to school and play. As kids we didn't always know the sacrifices he had to make. To appreciate how he helped raise us and all it might take.

Time went on and soon his boys were all grown, he was looking forward to enjoying some time of his own. But God had in his mind a different plan, that took my Dad way too soon. He was needed up in heaven, our hearts each shared that wound.

think of him often, and thank him for being my dad, still remember all the times that God allowed us to have. It is important for all to honor our dads and keep them close in your heart. Half of who you are is still him in part.

To all those who have a Dad up in heaven and miss him just like me, have faith he knows just how you feel and he will wait up for you and me.

# Times Flys

It's the end of June already and time keeps marching on, seems like the summer never lasts all that long. Christmas is coming exactly six months from here, we are just starting to feel the warmth of summer, not to notice that fall could be near.

Time goes by so fast when all the comes this time of year, but seems to drag along during all those snow storms we fear.

If only we could slow down the hands of time to enjoy these few months we receive, so our memories might make up for the six months of cold we soon will all perceive. Alas we live in New York, where the seasons are all well defined. Where the springs and summers are short, and the winters are seldom kind.

Although in between there exist a beauty during any season, something that makes you stay here for what most is a personal reason.

In the summer there are lakes that shimmer in the sun, for those who swim and fish there is a multitude of fun. In the fall we see colors that flood corners of your mind. We harvest the bounty of crops of every shape and kind. The winter does hold a special feel that all New Yorkers do hold, in that it takes a certain strength to endure all what may unfold. To see the empty frees fill up with a fresh white snow, can bring out an awesome feeling that only we will ever know.

Spring brings out a renewal to warm the souls that have long been chilled. The smell that flows through the air has our senses overfilled.

Now here we are toward the end of June, and Independence Day is coming soon. It is time to get out and enjoy mother earth, this cycle has been going on since the day of our birth. Another thought for today I give to my friends, as we live in this land where the never ends

# Marraige

For nearly fifty years I wandered the earth to find some meaning in my life. So, on this day eight years ago, I made someone my wife.

With deep brown eyes she looked up at me and simply said, I will. My days took on a whole new meaning as my prayers became fulfilled.

We share our time together now, as couples often do. We cheer each other up, when the other is feeling blue. Sleeping side by side to feel each other's touch. Always knowing from year to year we can still love each other that much.

She gave me a family when I thought those days were done. I have felt the love of our precious Grandson.

My lover, my best friend, had come to complete my soul at last. Our lives have grown from those vows that were cast. To my wife I give this piece of my heart, and like those words we spoke till death do us part.

Happy Anniversary my love, my Sue. These words came from deep inside, and were written just for you.

# Star Trek Tribute

Captain... Jim. Bones Doc.antibodies.poppycock. For those who understand these phrases I made, remember now before your memory fades.

These are a reference to a bold new time, when the human race was much more kind. Its' founder dreamed of a world united, a time when our efforts were not so damn short sighted.

To exist for the betterment of the human race, not to just fight over resources or emphasize a race.

Personal gain was not the reason to live, but to donate a skill, or service to give.

For those who have noticed the reference I have shown, perhaps you can share this philosophy well known.

Yes, I speak of a popular show, the creator I believe most of you will know. Gene Rodenberry was the man with this mission, a beautiful mind who sought a tame world with a vision.

This was something that could change what the world is today, a sensible place where our children could play. To unite the world as the human race, starts with recognizing our common face. We all bleed red, we are human to the core. It is only pure ignorance that makes us ignore.

A civilized man will understand these things, and perhaps appreciate the peace this could bring. A selfless approach to life can be key, to bring a calm outlook for the world to see, Would it not be rewarding as we each leave this world behind, that we left a better place for the next child to find.

# The Reunion

It's almost time to say goodbye to some old school chums I have known. We have laughed and told stories and reflected on how we have grown.

These times are precious as so many years have come to pass. The friendships we share will continue to last. Each time we meet there is a spark in our eyes, a flashback of our youth that never dies.

There is a sense of belonging that takes us back to a time, when the spirit of our neighborhood stood for pride, that this home was mine.

Many have moved on to start a family in another place, some of us have stayed while others vanished without a trace. One thing I know will always be true, as we live out the rest of our years. Is that the roots that we share and the bonds we have made, will live on through life's joys and fears.

We are a special group from an earlier time, when life made much more sense. Right was right, and wrong was wrong. There was not so much balancing on the fence.

Be proud my friends that we came from school where everyone knew your name. That no matter who you were, we were all treated the same. I see the same values that we were taught so long ago. We feel the same closeness we have all come to know.

Know in your hearts that where ever you may go, that there are folks that will always be family through these friendships we know. We share these things as we have grown up in the Heights, what our hearts know as home, to the warm familiar sights.

# A Positive View

Hello my friends, it is time now to shift. Realize that life is a beautiful gift. It is time to smile and laugh all we can, depression and the blues. I'm not a big fan.

Let's get together and have a good time with all the people we meet, go out and listen to music and make sure we move our feet.

Life is too short to do nothing less, as the earth moves by so fast, it is always important to establish those friendships that will endure and always last.

Do crazy things that will make you laugh as you tell your friends what you did. Reflect back on those same things you did when you were a kid.

Don't try to make sense of all the world throws at you only just enough to get you through.

Stress is something to avoid at all cost, it is only time and a portion of your life that will be lost.

Live large and enjoy every moment you can, and keep life as fresh as when it all just began.

This advise I give you because I wish to love all of mankind, these are the most relative words I think most anyone could find.

Trust that there is a positive place within us all, we only need to place ourselves outside of that negative wall. May I send you peace and a feeling of good, and that worldly contentment we could share if we only could.

# Tender Soul

They touch our hearts as we share our lives with those creatures so small and sweet. We get used to that feeling you have when they are curled up by your feet.

The friendly eyes that peer at you when you walk across the floor. The joy they feel when you come home from work, and you walk through that open door.

Most of all it's that warm body that pushes up next to yours, when you lay down to bed to close your eyes, it's that connection we all adore.

This is why it can hurt so much when these loved ones are called home so soon. God made their lives so short, and left an open wound.

Fear not my friend, as it has been claimed before, we will meet them on a bridge in time, your Pooh bear will purr in your arms and you both will be feeling fine.

This is the price we all must pay when we choose to bring them in our home. But the love we share with these creatures so pure will always keep us from being alone. Another soul will seek you out to take the place of your loss, but you will always know the time you had with him was always worth the cost.

Rest easy now, and think of him as a soft angel by your side. The life he lived was special because of the love he could never hide.

# Songs Of The Mind

Have you ever sat back and listen to a song that took you back in time? Back to an earlier part of your life when the sun always seemed to shine.

Music will take your mind to a place that will soothe your savage soul, back to that special feeling when your youth was still in control.

That guitarist you with fingers so fast, that driving rock that will always last. All of this reminds us of some happening in our lives, that song that was playing, sparked a memory inside, As our music is stored deep within our being, it becomes the eyes to our past we are seeing.

A bookmark to tag each year that had passed, perhaps a song to remember between the first and the last,

All I know is that each note can rule my day, from some driving rock to speed my heart, to a mellow jazz as I kneel down to pray.

Each style yields a frame of mind that can enhance every mood you control. The wonder of it all is how it can manipulate your soul.

Look back my friends on your all- time favorite song, as it puts you in a place that you know you belong. Let it take you there in that world called inner peace, and thank god that music is the ultimate feast,

# To My Mom

Thank you mom for helping make my life feel so complete. From giving all your good advice, to a lot of the cats beneath my feet. You have been my friend and so much more, I am blessed more than I know. I'm so lucky to have a Mom like you with all the kindness that you show. When I hear your name out around the town, it's mentioned with high regard, you have brought so much love to folks, when life can be so hard.

Thank you for all the times you've prayed for me Mom, I feel safer every day. It warms my heart to know that you care for me that way.
You're the best you know, an Angel sent from high above. For all these thin» you will always have n son's undying love. God sent you here to make this world a better place to live. The animals in his kingdom all know of the love you give. Always know how much you mean to us, whether be man or child or beast. No matter how bad the world might seem, we can be thankful for you, at least. I love you Mom and always will, cause you're the one who cares the most. The amount of joy you have given the world could stretch from coast to coast.

# Happy New Year

Here we are gathered around to celebrate another year past. Some of us are staying home while others go out and have a blast!

Thoughts go through our minds on how good or bad this year has been. Thinking of all the stuff in the news and the stories we have seen. Memories of this year gone by can be just a point of view. It depends on how much it all has changed with in the lives of me and you,

This perspective of time involves a glance at what other years have brought. A feeling of the things that we gained as compared to those dreams we all sought Sometimes we find a year fulfilled with much of what we planned, other times it all falls through like tiny grains of sand.

Whatever transpired in this year gone by makes little difference my friend. We made it through all the good and bad, and the next lies around the bend.

As these years fly by and we grow older you and l, our days take on deeper meanings as our nights slip quickly by. We look for brighter days in the new year to come, a special change that we know can happen to some.

Again, stress another point of view to give to all my friends. A relative thought that will bring you home, a message we could send. Our lives take on meaning when we live for the here and now. The year that has passed and the ones ahead are all less important somehow.

Enjoy each moment, each second in time as the next is promised to none. Love your mothers and fathers, all your daughters and sons. Live your life not to just wish for great things to come your way, but to love the life you were given to enjoy each and every day.

# *Dedicated To Gary Reynolds*

Listening to the world around me, knowing everything inside my head, not always able to speak too much, I smile at them instead. I remember younger days before, going fishing with my friends. Reflecting back when life was full, .....I remember when. My sister comes to see me, my wife and family too, wondering when all of this will change and I can be with all of you.

Time kept marching on, the days turned into years, I keep smiling all I can, never showing all my tears. I'm stronger now having passed the tests that life has given me. I've made the best of what has come, I've made my peace with

I see a light now, an awakening I have longed to feel. The pain I have been enduring is beginning now to heal.

My legs are strong and steady, my mind is crystal clear. I'm talking with mom and dad, there is nothing now I fear,

My life at times was difficult, but I lived the best I could. My youth was filled with all the things a man dreams that he should.

I met my wife and had a family, I worked hard to keep us strong I served my country as a soldier even though it felt so long.

Accepting what life has given has always been my style, I have met each day God has given me with my ever persistent smile. As I walk proud now with the Angels I give thanks now to you all. I am as strong as I have ever been, In heaven I'm standing tall!

• Gary Lee "Herb" Reynolds 11/04/1952 01/24/2016

# A Home For Us

A house is a home with its' roof over my head. There is a nice cozy kitchen, and upstairs of course, a bed. Rooms to lounge and watch TV, with all of this, a nice place to be.

But none of this would hold a meaning so true, if not for someone to share this, and honey, that person is you. That kitchen takes on the smell of home cooking, that seldom comes from my skills. We both work so hard together to make sure we pay all our bills.

Sometimes we watch TV in a totally separate place, but that's only because I like to watch people flying in outer space. When it gets late and we wander up to bed, there is still no one else next to I want to lay my head.

Our house is a home because we share our lives together this way. We look forward to each other's company as we strive to be happy, day by day. As we both get older and our priorities begin to change, we find that a simple existence is really not all that strange.

To understand that contentment of that roof over our heads, is much like the serenity we feel as we cuddle together in our bed. In the spring we plant flowers and enjoy campfires under the stars. We are thankful to God for all his earthly gifts thus far. Mostly I'm thankful on this Valentine's day for the woman who has made me feel this way. Because of a wife who makes me laugh, I can honestly say she's my better half.

# Motherhood

When we see the sparkle in our grandson's eyes and how sweet he has become, it's not hard to know how he came to be that way and his life has just begun.

He looks up to you as his loving support and is nourished by your caring hand. You have been so close to him since before he could stand. Most everything he is today is a reflection of the love you have shared.

He knows how safe and sound he is because of his mother's care. We thank you so deep in our hearts for raising such a beautiful son. It has so much to do with all the hard work you have done.

How lucky he is to have all the people that love him so much, please know how deeply our hearts have been touched. Without his love our lives would never be what they are today. Your love for him has blessed this boy in a very special way.

Be proud of what you have accomplished, it's not always easy what you have done. You have raised the sweetest boy and the most perf

# Memories

Here I am looking back, I can see the face's but maybe the names I lack.

I was young then, with the strength like no other, not knowing that someday I would become someone's mother.

My life was so intense as I danced across the nation, nothing would compare to that awesome sensation. From the grounds of the state fair to the stage at a theater so bright, I was alive with the music that orchestrated my flight.

But alas, I was destined to give birth to some wonderful son's, my days of dancing are now memories along by the many travels I have done.

Many years have passed as I have started a new life, I have good husband, he has made me his wife. But along came a time when God took him away, and now life has changed, how I wished he could stay.

My boys are still here and I don't feel so all alone, I have my faith, and a comfortable home. I started to work so to continue my life, although never to be someone else's wife.

I traveled the world to see what God had created, the people I met seemed to all be related. The world seemed smaller then, when I returned to my home. But once again I was living alone.

I then found a love that was lasting and so much better than that, as I embraced the comfort of a faithful cat. Soon I found a few more in need, I brought them into my home to feed.

This is why God brought me into my life, to care for the innocent, to understand their strife.

Now my life is so much harder it seems, my younger days dominate my dreams. I think of all the things I could do when I was young, All the people I knew, the songs I have sung.

I wait now, to see what God wants me to do. The love for my boys' and my cats are so true.

I am still strong in my mind and my spirit flies like a bird, but I'm waiting dear Lord to hear your blessed word.

These are the thoughts that my mom has been expressing to me over the last few months. I needed to write them down, as they were fresh in my memory. I know she might not have the chance to get to a keyboard, but you may be surprised. My family is hoping that she will be with us for a long time yet, however her health as of late has been slowing down. Prayers will help.

# A Cat's life

I wake up in the morning, because I hear my master stir;
Brushing up against his leg, I let out a real loud purr. I follow
him down the stairs to the kitchen we will go;
I meow once or twice "I'm hungry", just to let him know.
He scoops something out of a metal can, I see;
I'm sure that's some food he's scooping out for me. Yes! I was
right, I'm not going to budge, as he puts down my dish, I give
him a little nudge.
I look up at my master, and with my best voice,
Hey you idiot, I wanted Sea Captains Choice! "I guess it
won't matter, this isn't so bad, it's a whole lot fresher than
the last stuff I had.
So, I eat it all up and run down the stairs, because I feel this
urge to relieve myself there.
After that's done I'm ready for action, I'll go fight with my
brother for some quick satisfaction. Soon however, I find
myself weak, and a nice warm lap is the comfort I seek.
I found my master, he's watching TV, I'm sure he won't mind
petting the likes of me.
I lay on his lap and tuck my feet in, I feel so warn, soon my
nap will begin.
Before you know it it's dinner again, and I put on my lovey
face to con my human friend.
As he pats me on the head, and says come on follow me; I
know it's a cat's life I'll always want to be.

# Springtime

Remember when all the grass was green, the trees were full and streets were clean? These are the days I wish for now, I see the cold winds are blowing; there goes the snow plow.

I long for a time when the sun heats my soul; these long winter days are taking their toll. Day turns to darkness too soon and it's also true, that winter- time can make you blue.

Bring me those days when night falls real late, walking with the sun on my back, I just can't wait.

Bring me those days of blue skies and gentle breezes, far from the times when the chill is in the air, and everything freezes.

Remember the smell of fresh cut lawns as you pass on by, the bell on the ice cream truck rings as you watch the robins fly. These are the days I long for. It's too cold to go outside, makes me want to climb under my covers and hide.

I long for a time to escape from my cave, to climb out to a meadow and run through a field, to walk out in a lake and feel a warm wave.

Bring me those days when night falls real late, walking with the sun on my back, I just can't wait.

Bring me those days of blue skies and gentle breezes, far from the times when the chill is in the air, and everything freezes.

# Spirits Surround Us

The earth bounding through the emptiness of space, she carries the essence of the human race. Around the Milky Way we ride the endless ride. A powerful force that will never subside.

Together with all the human spirits that lived, and still live; We exist as an energy through only the Creator can give. Likewise, the stars and the moons up above, owe their existence to his undying love.

No man can stop what has been put into motion, nor can he stop us from spinning, or drain all the oceans.

So, we should all take this ride on our ship called Mother earth, as brothers and sisters that know what it's worth.

The universe is vast and the heavens unknown, it is best to live together than to exist all alone.

Matthew D. Cook 2004

# Dream Girl

My search is over as I recognize fate, I know that no longer should I look for a date.

I've found a woman so tender and sweet, so much of the one I've dreamed someday I'd meet.

We share the same feelings and feel so secure, whenever we are close, of this I am sure.

Everything about her just fits like a glove, with her I can share the true meanings of love.

Wherever life takes us I know we will find a knowledge of a true peace of mind.

This woman I have found is my most perfect match, and not to mention, one hell of a catch.

Her beautiful eyes and incredible smile cast a spell on me so intense, that being her man is something that will always make sense. I thank the Lord and Bonnie for bringing us near, and I will strive for as long as she wants me, and hold her so dear.

# With Love To My Bride

A year has gone by since I asked for your hand, a tear as I placed on your wedding band.

I know in my heart you are the love of my life, as I will cherish you always as my beloved wife.

The time will go by now, and with each passing day, I will always remind you that I still feel this way. You are my strength that gets me through each year that I live, and it will be my heart and soul that I will always give.

We are married now as we enjoy our first Christmas as one, each of us loving what this marriage has done, we have brought together two souls that were always meant to be, and pledged our love throughout eternity. For you my love, I give you this thought, to remember this Christmas and all the meaning it has brought.

I LOVE YOU

# To My Sue

As we enter this time of year my sweet, there is something I know is true. That I'm so thankful to have my life made brighter by a woman as kind as you. I have never met someone so sweet with a heart that's made of gold. When I need someone to warm my soul, it's you 1 want to hold. You're the thought that comes to mind when I lay down my weary head, and the very first thing I think about when I climb up out of bed. Our lives were enhanced my love, when we met that summers day. As the seasons pass this will not change, our love will pave the way. Thank you Sue for giving me a gift that keeps on giving. Your presence in my world sure makes life feel more like living.

Go forward through each day my love with faith I'll always be near. It's the way you make me feel inside that keeps me close, my dear.

# The Spirit Within

What is this presence within yourself that makes you believe you're alive? A spark or awareness that continues along no matter if you think about it or not, I feel this presence as I think to myself, as too often I find myself alone. I'm relating to someone my thoughts and experiences as if to be consumed in conversation. Decisions I make are tossed back and forth as if it were a debate. To whom am I asking or confiding if not my own soul, or an inner being other than what is conceived on the outside as myself. These are the questions I ask in the same manner, to find out if I am indeed alone, or sharing existence with a spirit inside other than my own. Could this be the spirit of God in which we are all in tuned to accept within? A person to ask questions of the heart, and expect correct answers, even. though we may not ourselves be intelligent enough to answer. Or do we accept our own decisions as correct only from the experiences we have had through trial and error with all of life's experiences brought together. This makes me wonder if truth is universal in respect to an inner instinct, much like our animal friends, that determines out conception of right and wrong. Coded in our DNA the countless years of man's existence stored in the depths of our minds. To say to yourself, "I think, therefore I am", can be attributed to a combination of your own human spirit* and the accumulated experiences of everyone born before you. Deep inside are the answers awaiting me that are all set down by a higher being that started the big bang in the first place. Namely God.

Still, as I sit in wonderment on how I can carry on a conversation in my mind with myself, I can only come to the conclusion that two entities exist within. This is more than likely where the expression" you are your own best friend" came from in the first place. The one spirit is indeed my own, while the other is also myself as a reflection of the pieces of my heritage, as well- as personality traits from many family members from past times as well as present ones. To find strength within, is to tap the DNA codes of all humans before me all the way back to the creator himself. In this matter, time can indeed stand still, and be brought together as one in the realms of time and space. This reasoning in which I have laid down here, can be assumed has been reasoned time and again by many men before me, and will be passed down long after I am lifted to a higher plane of existence. Therefore, a cycle of existence is revealed through a certain logic to all of this. A message of truth can be found by listening to the other spirit inside of us all. I feel better already! Have a great day to the spirits in all of us.     By Matthew Cook 2003

# Kill or Be Killed

Kill or be killed, is that the name of the game?
Are we looking for just another reason to fight, or someone else to blame.
This is not the answer my friend, and by now we all should know; That killing each other is a sin no matter where the oil will flow.

How can we justify a war that won't be won, by lining up all the people we hate in front of a loaded gun.
As civilized men, we should wish to improve the way in which we live.
To think a lot less of what we can take, and figure out what we can give.

We are the only kind of life on this earth that hunts down ourselves- it's insane; So, what makes us think we can claim to be human, when we can't even be humane, Peace on this earth can only be found if we all can exist as one.
As the people of earth, we are all the same, let this be spoken loudly, let the wars be done.

# Traveling Man

Hello my love, I'm off again to travel across the land Always ever mindful of this ring on my hand. I know each day that passes, I'll miss you more and more.

Looking forward to that point in time when I walk back in the door.

The spring air has returned again and reminds us of our love, how fresh and warm our hearts remain and as vast as the sky above.

You are the strength that helps me through each day in my journey through life, I'm proud to be the lucky man who has such a wife.

Sleep well my sweet and think of me as you close those sexy eyes. I'll be doing the same many miles away and as we both let out a sigh.

# With Love To My Bride

A year has gone by since I asked for your hand, a tear as I placed on your wedding band.

I know in my heart you are the love of my life, as I will cherish you always as my beloved wife.

The time will go by now, and with each passing day, I will always remind you that I still feel this way. You are my strength that gets me through each year that I live, and it will be my heart and soul that I will always give. We are married now as we enjoy our first Christmas as one. Each of us loving what this marriage has done. We have brought together two souls that were always meant to be, and pledged our love throughout eternity. For you my love, I give you this thought, to remember this Christmas and all the meaning it has brought.

I LOVE YOU

# The Colon Poem

They put me in this little room, with these special little pants. Around the room the nurses loomed, as if they were doing a dance.

Soon I felt a little dizzy and then a smile on my face, as I saw everything moving kind of slow looking around the place.

Lean over on your side he said, with sinister kind of tone. You might feel a little pinch, as I let out a little moan.

What channel is this, I thought as I was watching some strange TV.

That sure looks somewhat like a personal part of me.

By now I knew I wasn't in bed with my lovely little, wife. But instead I was getting the deepest reaming of my whole entire life!

Soon after this I looked up to see my doctor wasn't all that mean, when he looked down at me and said "Boy, your squeaky clean!" They sent me to another room to get rid of some excess gas, I had to do some funny moves to make all that pass.

Then off went to the nearest sub shop to get me something to eat.

One of those foot- long pulled pork subs was my special treat. My ordeal is over, and it's good to know that all is well up there, but 10 years from now when they ask me again I'll be telling them I just don't care.

# Troubled Times

As I exist in my world at peace here at home. I listen to news in dismay. It seems that elsewhere it is not the same, as they are thinking in a different way.

I've always thought after thousands of years that man would evolve in his mind, to think in a way that would allow everyone to respect and love all mankind.

This is not the case as I watch all this hate and greed, as I see all the children we neglect to feed.

Instead of improving our quality of life, the world seems to be forgetting the quest, to look into each of our souls and bring out only the best.

Too many souls are lost each day in the name of selfish desires. To many chances are missed each day to put out all these senseless fires.

Perhaps it's time to join a force more powerful than each other, to give a chance for peace and get along with one another. All this killing in the world is an example of a real lack of purpose. What we see on the news is just scratching the surface.

All of the effort taken to remove someone's life or land, could be used to improve life instead of useless bombs in the sand.

These simple ideas are as old as time. that have been in the thoughts of yours and mine. But how to convince those people of hate may be the beginning of everyone's fate.

We claim to be so technically advanced as we can send men to the moon, I only wish that we could find a way to peace and do it real soon!

Printed in the United States
By Bookmasters